IMAGES
of England

HEART OF ENGLAND
FAIRS

The Lord Mayor of Coventry (Councillor Winslow) performs the official opening of Coventry Whit Fair, 1958.

IMAGES
of England

HEART OF ENGLAND
FAIRS

Compiled by
Vanessa Toulmin, Julie Campbell,
Graham Downie and Ian Trowell

TEMPUS

First published 2000
Copyright © Vanessa Toulmin, Graham Downie, Julie Campbell
and Ian Trowell, 2000

Tempus Publishing Limited
The Mill, Brimscombe Port,
Stroud, Gloucestershire, GL5 2QG

ISBN 0 7524 2076 3

Typesetting and origination by
Tempus Publishing Limited
Printed in Great Britain by
Midway Clark Printing, Wiltshire

Jack Leeson.

Contents

Dwarfed by the Gallopers of William Bagnall, there three youngsters wait for a ride at Leicester's Saffron Lane Fair on 10 May 1958.

Introduction

The Heart of England Fairs and the Jack Leeson Collection

Jack Leeson was born in Long Buckby, Northamptonshire, in 1920, where regular visits to the local fair inspired his lifelong fascination with everything to do with the fairground. After training as an engineer, he settled in Rugby with his wife Win and their daughter Jacqueline, where he started to pursue what would be a forty-year-long passion for photographing the visits of travelling fairs to the Midlands. His first recorded picture was of Fletcher's Ark taken at Rugby Fair in June 1949 and this was soon followed by visits to Leicester in October 1950 and May 1951, Long Buckby in May 1951 and Sutton Coldfield in July 1951.

Over the following decades he took almost 8,000 photographs including annual visits to Loughborough, Oxford, Stratford and many other famous historic fairs associated with the region. Over the years, Jack secured some wonderful photographs of various firms including Joe Stevens, Billy Danter and Bob Wilson. He and his fellow enthusiasts would meet at events organized by the now defunct Friendship Circle of Showland Fans and he began lifelong friendships with fellow photographers Rowland Scott and Philip Bradley. In a tribute published in the *Mercury*, the journal of the Fairground Association of Great Britain, his friend Rowland Scott penned the following words:

My memories go back to the many happy hours we spent at the Nottingham draw on and especially to that historic day on September 23, 1958, when for the first and only time Jack, Philip Bradley and myself were on the same ground together. The location was the now defunct Serpentine site at Aston, the long time home of the Birmingham Onion Fair. All three of us had our cameras constantly clicking, recording the arrival of the loads and the rides being assembled.

Jack photographed a wide range of subjects which included the setting up of the fair, general views, full views and close-ups of machines, shows, fairground folk, publicity and customs

Philip Bradley and Rowland Scott in front of J. Cartwright's refreshment van on the day they met up with Jack Leeson.

and ceremonies associated with a particular event, such as the ox-roasting at Stratford-upon-Avon Mop. In photographing these scenes, Jack captured images of cultural and social history, and the humanity of the resulting photographs reflect Jack's own unique personality. The photographs were taken all over the Midlands and elsewhere over a period of forty years, using a comparatively simple camera, and Jack printed his monochrome negatives meticulously, hand-shading in his enlarger to get good gradation.

After his death in January 1995, Jack's daughter Jacqueline deposited the collection in the newly formed National Fairground Archive, based in the University Library, Sheffield. The archive was founded in 1994 after an approach was made by the Fairground Association of Great Britain in order to house, preserve, conserve and provide access to the wealth of material relating to travelling fairs and showpeople in the United Kingdom. Since that auspicious day, the collections have grown from strength to strength, and the National Fairground Archive can today claim to be the leading repository of material relating to British fairs and the amusement industry. Its current holdings include a wide variety of documents, over 1,000 books on the history of popular entertainment, posters, handbills and hundreds of hours of audio-visual material, which record not only the history of fairs and popular entertainment but the essential and previously overlooked role played by travelling showpeople. One of the most important aspects of the collection are the 60,000 photographs, a substantial portion of which were taken by members of the Fairground Association and include the Ron Taylor, Jack Leeson and Rowland Scott Collections. They date from the 1880s to the present day and reflect the variety of venues and locations associated with fairs in the United Kingdom over the past 120 years. All of these collections are currently being catalogued and will be made available as a digital catalogue, with the Jack Leeson collection alone consisting of approximately 11,600 photographs and negatives, both collected and taken by him. The information contained within the Leeson collection is invaluable and, along with Jack's notebooks that were also donated by the family, contain detailed lists of every fair visited by him over forty years. An elaborate system of cross-referencing enables the researcher to match the photograph and Jack's account of the fair, along with a detailed listing of the showpeople who were in attendance. One of Jack's notebooks (number 5) contains the following description of Clifton Wakes Fair, dated 11 September 1959:

Win and I walked to Clifton on a lovely warm and close evening. We found A. Barker's fair in the sports field near the school. Machines were Barker's Dodgem and Ark, Fossett's Juvenile with Chiappa Organ, Fossett's boats, Warwick's shooter and the usual array of stalls and hooplas.

Then he continues:

The shooter side panels have been very nicely touched up. A. Fossett is connected with the circus people and mainly travels in the Staffordshire area. On the speakers – Living Doll – Cliff Richard. Left fair about 8.30 and called at Lower Road Fish Shop and took fish and chips home for supper. Home 9.30 p.m.

Jack's training as an engineer also resulted in an ability to describe the mechanical principles of riding devices with simple freehand sketches, supported by only a few written words, and these diagrams are much in evidence throughout his notebooks.

The Jonah the Whale show at Rugby Spring Fair, March 1954.

A brief introduction to Heart of England Fairs

Jack Leeson visited many fairs over the forty years, which, for the purposes of this book, are split into the following eight sections (nine counties and cities in all): Warwickshire, Northamptonshire, Oxfordshire, Gloucestershire, Herefordshire and Worcestershire, Leicestershire, Coventry, and Birmingham.

One distinctive feature of the fairs at the Heart of England region is the large number that are still held on the original town centre sites. Indeed, within the eight areas featured in this book there are more street fairs than in any other part of the country, with around twenty-five fairs held by charter or ancient custom occupying market places and village greens. Many of these can be traced to the fourteenth century and the passing of the Statute of Labourers in 1351 by Edward III. These Statute fairs, or Mops as they are known in the Midlands, still continued in their original purpose of hiring until the end of the nineteenth century. However, even with these hiring fairs, the original purpose of the event was soon superseded by the amusements and many of these fairs continue as pleasure fairs today. These include the Mop Fairs held in Studley, Stratford, Warwick and Tewkesbury for example, that all owe their existence and continuation as fairs to the original hiring fairs of many years ago.

Jack Leeson's home town of Rugby enjoyed as many as five different fairs throughout the travelling season, with a visit from the Armstrong family as early as March. However, the season really got into swing at Easter, with big fairs at Birmingham, Coventry, and Northampton. The month of May saw several big fairs again at Coventry and Nuneaton, before the summer allowed the travelling fairground families to plot their courses through the smaller towns and villages of the Heart of England. Jack Leeson's central position in Rugby allowed him to document most of the comings and goings across this large region, keeping a visual record of changes in machinery, transport and personalities. After paying his customary visits to Long Buckby and Rugby for the August fairs, Leeson concentrated on the feverish Autumn activity signalled by the classic St Giles Fair held in Oxford. September was concluded by another famous large event, Birmingham Onion Fair, and October was characterized by Michaelmas Fairs at Stratford-upon-Avon, Warwick, Daventry and Banbury. Following the bonfire fairs the season was normally concluded with the large street fair at Loughborough.

One very famous street fair is Oxford St Giles Fair, which takes place on the first Monday after the first Sunday following the feast of St Giles (September 1) and lasts for two days.

The rights to hold the fair at St Giles are shared between St John the Baptist College, Oxford, and the local council, and the fair itself is opened by the Lord Mayor of Oxford at 10.30 on the Monday morning. The showfamilies arrive early on the Sunday morning and the pull on starts for the larger machines at 6.00a.m., followed by the juveniles and fun houses at 7.30a.m., and kiosks and side stalls building up from 9.00a.m. onwards. History reveals that this was not always the case; up until 1851 the showpeople started to congregate at midnight on the Saturday in readiness for the fair on the following Monday. With today's fair the building up continues throughout Sunday with a break for an hour from 12.00 noon till 1.00p.m. for Sunday service. Oxford, in line with many of the historic fairs featured in this book, has a long pedigree, and over the years many claims have been made regarding the ancestry of the famous Oxford St Giles Fair. H.L. Benwell writing in *The Showman* in 1906 claims an ancient lineage, stating that: 'The Oxford Fair is of Norman origin but its actual beginnings are lost in the mists of antiquity'. In this article Benwell linked the modern festivities to the medieval fair held in the manor of Walton where it took place on the 'precincts of the churchyard itself on St Giles Day

Oxford St Giles Fair is held on the first Monday following the first Sunday after the feast of St Giles (1 September) and lasts for two days. Shows were an important element of the travelling fair as this photograph, taken in 1928, illustrates. Members of the Chipperfield family, of circus and fairground fame, are seen presenting their dancing in the lion den act, where a lady lion tamer would dance in the cages with the lions.

and the following week'. However, despite the story, there appears to be no documentary evidence that a fair was held there during the medieval period. The fair itself is historically divided between the 'college' and the 'city' side, with the college side tracing its rights to the fair from the Manor of Walton. The west side of the fair falls beyond these boundaries and as the fair expanded in the Victorian period, the Markets and Fairs Committee took the initiative of collecting tolls for this area. This practise is still maintained today under the co-ordination and management of the Property and Leisure Department of the City Council.

Jack visited Oxford from 1955 to 1971 and photographed the range of amusements on offer which included Dodgems, Swirls, Autodromes, Juvenile Rides including swings and double-decker buses and a multitude of side stalls and hooplas provided by long term tenants such as the Hatwell, Buckland, Pickard and Rawlins families. During the 1950s Oxford continued to attract both visitors and the latest rides and novelties, presented by the showmen: John Flanagan was there with his Autodrome, the Traylen Brothers presented their Helter-Skelter and Dive Bomber and Harry Studt continued his family's connection with the fair with his Brookland Speedway. During the following decade, a whole range of attractions attended the fair, with shows and novelty stalls proving to be as popular as ever. The showrow contained such delights as Tom Norman with Takala and his Red Indian Troupe, Billy Raynor's Mouseland Circus, Mrs Jack Gage's boxing and wrestling show and Mrs Sonia Allen with the Crocodile Girl, the Chimpanzee Circus and Nyora the Rat Girl. By 1966 Bob Wilson's thrilling Trabant ride was the major new attraction at the fair, providing an interesting contrast to the Hatwell family shooter which had been attending St Giles for over seventy years. Over the past forty years change has become a common feature of the modern fairground, with the general public demanding more innovative and thrill seeking entertainment. The residents of Oxford have seen a wide variety in the range of rides, shows and amusements brought by the showpeople to what is widely claimed to be the best street fair in Europe and these were captured faithfully by Jack during his annual visit to the September fair.

Another famous street fair, heavily featured in Jack's collection, is Loughborough Charter Fair, acknowledged to be the last major established fair of the season, and a selection of images from this fair have been chosen from nearly 200 taken by Jack over the years. Over the past seven centuries the relationship between the local people and the November fair has survived, despite various attempts to move the festivities to the outskirts of the town. Like any Charter Fair, Loughborough has a long, rich and varied history. The original Charter, granted in 1221 and pertaining to an annual event on 31 July, was reaffirmed seven years later and extended to cover

Annie Holland's Living Wagon with Palace of Delight Cinematograph Show photographed in 1911. Mrs Annie Holland are her two children Maud Holland and Bertie can be seen on the wagon steps as they take a break while on the road. Annie Holland's cinematograph show could reputedly hold 1,000 people and travelled throughout the Midlands from 1898 until the outbreak of the First World War.

three days around the Feast of St Peter. A third Charter was granted in 1228 by Henry III to Hugh Le Despenser, Lord of the Manor of Loughborough, and related to the Feast of All Souls. The changes to the Calendar introduced in 1752 resulted in the loss of eleven days and the date of the fair became the 13 November. However, in 1881 local officials obtained an order to stipulate that the opening day of the Fair would always fall on the second Thursday in November and that date has since remained constant. The showfamilies associated with Loughborough Fair from this period are still familiar to present-day fairgoers and include famous names such as Collins, Proctor, Hall, Richards and the Holland family, who first attended the fair in the days of the bioscope show presented by Mrs Annie Holland.

The arrival of cinema in the form of the bioscope in 1897 had been preceded by the annual visit of Wall's Phantoscope from the 1880s and the popularity of the shows, which included G. Chadwick's Giant Octopus and Vampire Girl show, V. Jeffrey's Dracula's Daughter show, Billy Wood's Boxing Booth and E. Munro's Rat Girl show, continued in the twentieth century. Loughborough Fair, like many of its counterparts, was closed for the duration of the First World War and only opened again after hostilities ceased. By the 1920s the showmen were introducing the latest attractions to entice the local fairgoers with the arrival of the Globe of Death and the Wall of Death in 1929. However, the fair attracted its usual dissenters with some commentators describing it 'as a Fair with a mile of caravans ... that ... should be removed from our streets', reflecting the now familiar argument over the disruption caused to motorists due to the loss of parking for the duration of the fair. However, the people of Loughborough remained loyal to the tradition of their street fair and it still remains on its historic site.

Jack Leeson first visited Loughborough Fair in the early 1950s when it had become one of the main fairs of the year for showpeople and locals alike. A *World's Fair* reporter wrote in 1955 that the event was really five fairs held in various locations and linked together by stalls, games and juvenile machines in the streets adjoining. Attractions included John Farrar's modern Waltzer, Charles Thurston's Skid and Henry Armstrong's Caterpillar and alloy Dodgems. Ten years later the fair underwent another change with the whole of the Market Place given over to amusements, resulting in the fair attaining greater prominence in the town centre. Over the following years the fair continued to adapt and develop in line with the improvements taking place on fairgrounds around the country, as the showpeople continued to invest in new equipment and constantly provide the latest in high speed technology and innovation, all aspects of which were captured and documented by Jack Leeson. In the last few years fairs have been returning to the streets, with Worcester and Hinckley seeing the return of fairground amusements to the centres of their towns.

Pat Collins

Many of the fairs photographed by Jack Leeson were associated with, or attended by, the famous Collins family, with the present day firm still based in the Midlands. The majority of the fairs photographed by Jack Leeson would have been part of the Pat Collins circuit with his heir John Collins running the events during the 1950s. Although many famous showfamilies have attended fairs for generations in the Heart of England, the name of Pat Collins is truly synonymous with the areas photographed by Leeson. Pat Collins was born in Chester on 12 May 1859, and for the majority of his professional life as a showman he was based and associated with the Midlands. By the time of his death in 1943, Pat Collins had become the most successful showman of his generation, both on and away from the fairground. His achievements

An aerial view of Pat Collins' machines at Coventry Whit Fair in 1928. Attractions on show include: the Scenic Railway and the Razzle Dazzle both popular machines of the time.

included being the longest serving President of the Showmen's Guild of Great Britain, the biggest lessee on the fairgrounds and proprietor of nearly every type of roundabout manufactured. He served as a member of Walsall Borough Council, including a term as mayor – and was the town's Member of Parliament for three years. However, as his time as a politician illustrates, his activities and impact extended beyond the fairground fraternity and he also went on to build up a chain of over thirteen cinemas, theatres and skating rinks in Birmingham and the Midlands. His association with the region began in the 1880s and by 1882 he had become based in Walsall and attended Bloxwich Wakes with an unspecified ride. In the following years he went from strength to strength, buying the land he first leased and renaming it Gondola Works, and becoming the owner of various roundabouts. This success was further consolidated by the acquisition of sites for the running of fairs and Pat Collins was the sole lessee of numerous fairs in the Black Country and the famous Birmingham Onion Fair.

In the late 1890s Pat Collins was one of, if not, the leading roundabout proprietors in the country and by 1900 he had expanded his business yet again to incorporate the latest innovation on the travelling fairs, the cinematograph show. By the mid-1920s, Pat Collins claimed to own fourteen cinemas or assorted variety establishments. These included three cinemas in the Black Country, of which the Grosvenor in Bloxwich is the only one still remaining; the purpose built Cinema De Luxe in Chester; and the Waldorf Skating Ring in Birmingham.

Pat Collins held the office of President of the Showmen's Guild from 1909 until 1929 when he retired after twenty years, with the honour of being its longest serving President. In 1918 he was co-opted as Councillor for the Birchills Ward in Walsall, his adopted home town, but soon developed more of a taste for political life. He was elected the Member of Parliament for the borough of Walsall in November 1922 when he was returned as the Liberal candidate with a majority of 325. This was increased the following year when he was re-elected with a majority of over 2,000 votes. Unfortunately Pat's true potential was never fully realized as his term only lasted another year when he was defeated in the 1924 General Election by the Conservative candidate W. Preston. Pat Collins continued to serve as a Councillor in the borough and became an Alderman in 1930. As his political life continued, his amusement concerns continued to develop and expand as his son Pat, or Young Pat as he was known, became more and more involved in the family business. Pat Collins had examples of nearly all of the popular and innovative rides travelling, and employed managers who travelled all of his major machines throughout the Midlands and beyond.

In 1938 he was elected Mayor of Walsall and it is believed he was offered a Knighthood by Chamberlain, an honour he declined on the grounds that he had been born plain Pat Collins and would die the same. He died on 8 December 1943 and his death was greeted with sorrow

Pat Collins, 'King of Showmen', and undoubtedly the most successful roundabout proprietor, lessee of this day. President of the Showmen's Guild from 1909 until 1929, he also achieved high office outside the fairground fraternity, including Member of Parliament for Walsall in 1922, and was also Lord Mayor and Alderman of the town.

and shock on fairgrounds throughout the United Kingdom. He had reigned supreme in the Midlands and beyond for most of the first half of the century and his name had become synonymous with fairs in the Midlands. So extensive did his business become that at its peak he was running as many as four fairs a week as well as attending such major fairs as Hull, Nottingham and Newcastle. These events and fairs continued after his death but no one showman could again dominate such a large section of the country.

The photographs which make up *Heart of England Fairs* are only a small fraction of the thousands of images that make up the Jack Leeson collection. The images we have chosen for this book reflect both Jack's fascination with the mechanical history of the fair and his skill as a photographer in capturing the whole experience and merriment that the annual fair brings to a town or village. What follows is a selection of Jack's photographs which are representative of the collection as a whole. Rather than selecting by Fair, the selection follows the counties that make up the Heart of England and include photographs of the now defunct Birmingham Onion Fair in all its glory, the Mop fairs that take place in Stratford, Warwick and Tewkesbury, to name but a few, and the famous Charter Fairs visited by Jack on numerous occasions. Jack's shrewd vision has left us with a rich legacy that stands as a unique record of the fairgrounds of a generation. Although a percentage of these photographs have appeared in fairground magazines they have never been seen by the people who actually attended the fairs in the Heart of England. With the publication of this book, it is hoped that the photographic legacy that is the Jack Leeson Collection will now be more widely available.

Dr Vanessa Toulmin
Research Director
National Fairground Archive
University Library
University of Sheffield
For further information regarding the National Fairground Archive and its holdings please visit our web site at http://www.shef.ac.uk/uni/projects/nfa

One
Warwickshire

The most famous of Warwickshire's fairs is Stratford Mop, held in the streets of the Bard's home town on 12 October. This day of 'merry-making and frolic' was once popular over a wide area of the Midlands. In the heyday of the railways, 'Moppers' would arrive at Stratford by the thousand, carried there by special excursion trains. The Mop was once a hiring, or Statute fair. In the days before the advent of labour exchanges, farmworkers could seek fresh employment each Michaelmas at these hiring fairs. Small emblems worn in their clothing denoted their particular trade: the shepherd would sport a tuft of wool, the carter a piece of whipcord, the thatcher a tassle of straw. It was these tokens – known as 'mops' – that earned the hirings their nickname. The term is peculiar to those counties in and around the Cotswolds. Many of the Mops were followed a week or so later by a second hiring – the 'Runaway Mop'. Labourers who found that their new position was not all they had bargained for would 'run away' to try for a more congenial job at the second gathering. Stratford still preserves this tradition, with its Runaway Mop taking place on the second Friday after the first fair.

A general view of Rugby Rag Fair as seen from the Railway Terrace, 3 September 1960.

Fellow enthusiasts, left to right: Les Chater, Jim Miles, Midge Chater and Fred Richardson about to explore Rugby Spring Fair in March 1959. Jack Leeson regularly met other fairground fans to exchange photographs and share information.

Robert Brothers' elephants, with Johnny Robert walking alongside, head the parade along Murray Road to signal the arrival of the circus in April 1962.

18

A rainy lunch break in September allows Leeson to capture this view of the 1965 Rugby Rag Fair. Barker's Octopus and Thompson's Lighthouse Slip are both prominent.

Chicken Joe's Striker forms part of Stevens' Rugby Fair in May 1960. A popular test of strength amongst the town's youth, Strikers provided an opportunity for punters to make an impression on the onlooking crowd.

C. Morris' Big Wheel towers over Warwick Market Place as Leeson photographs the pull-down of the Mop Fair on Sunday 23 October 1966.

Wally Shufflebottom's Strip Tease Show caught in all its decorative glory on 18 October 1958 at Warwick Mop Fair. Leeson notes that 'Arthur and I patronized the show and were given a first rate exhibition of knife and hatchet throwing by Wally'. Wally Shufflebottom was the youngest son of William Benjamin Shufflebottom a Wild West and Buffalo Bill impersonator who performed under the name of Texas Bill in the 1880s. Wally first travelled his show in the 1930s and continued until the 1970s when he was one of the last showmen to present live entertainment on the fairground.

Brewer's Juvenile Dobbies and Motor Cars at Warwick Mop Fair photographed 18 October 1958.

The dismantling of N.B. Davies' Dodgem track attracts interest from a passing cyclist as he crosses Warwick Market Place on 23 October 1966.

'Ted' photographed on the centre island of Barker's Ark at Leamington May Fair, 13 May 1961. Leeson writes about having lunch at 'Bobby's Restaurant' and paying 2½d bus fare from Leicester Street to Campion Hill, where the fair was held.

C. Cotton's thirty-six-seater Chairoplanes photographed at rest at Leamington May Fair, 13 May 1961.

Elias Harris' Wall of Death stirs up some interest as the paraders and spielers tempt passers-by with a taste of what the paying punter will see. This photograph taken at Rugby Rag Fair in June 1950. The Wall of Death first appeared on the fairground in 1929 where it was an immediate sensation. Part of the many tricks the dare devil riders used to perform include riding on the handlebars of the Indian motorbikes, standing on the seat and attaching a side car to the bike that could carry passengers. One of the tricks Elias Harris was famous for was riding the wall with a lion as a passenger in the sidecar.

P. Danter's Overboats, with Mrs Danter in charge at Rugby Rag Fair, 2 September 1961. This ride was eventually perserved by the late Jeff Bach and remains the only working example.

Rugby crowds around a Brandy Snap Stall at the 1956 Summer Fair. Brandy Snap still remains a popular fairground confectionery.

A group of showmen –
including Messrs Cooper,
Connell, Warwick and
Merrin – relax on the steps
of Barker's Ark during a
quiet moment at the 1961
Summer Fair.

Publicity posters for
Stevens' 1960 Fair pasted
onto Rugby Cattle Market
wall.

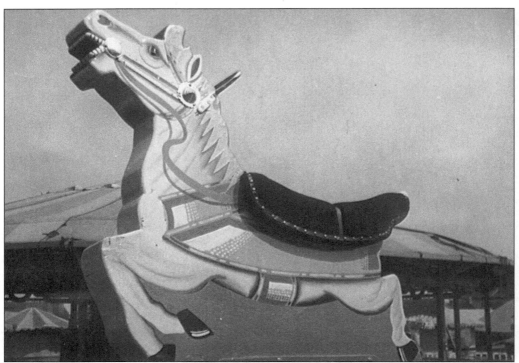

A mount from J. Stevens' Maxwell built Ark. The Ark was new in 1958 and open for only the third time when Leeson took this photograph on Rugby Cattle Market. In the later years many Arks were built or re-fitted with motorbikes and travelled as 'Easyriders'.

Stevens' Fair photographed 8 June 1963, on Rugby Market Place. The Ark can be seen with its 'Sputnik Chaser' front, reflecting the change in interest from 1950s science fiction to 1960s science fact as the race into space began in earnest.

Crowds gather in spite of the rain for the civic opening of the 1958 Stratford-upon-Avon Mop Fair. Leeson notes that, 'The town crier bade silence for the Mayor who opened this ancient Statute Mop Fair. A reply was made by Billy Bagnall on behalf of the Guild, and he invited the Mayor to sample any of the amusements. The opening was on the stroke of 11.00a.m.'. Deakin's superb Lakin built Ark fills the background, this machine being a popular attraction amongst the back-end fairs. The Ark still travels, although now as a Waltzer. After passing through various owners it was redecorated in a traditional style by Oxfordshire based showman Harry Hebborn. The rights to hold a Fair in Stratford-upon-Avon were granted in 1216 to be held on the eve, day and morrow of 29 October, the patronal festival of Holy Trinity Church. However, the Mop fair traces its ancestry in the Statute of Labourers in 1351, with 12 October being Stratford Mop Day. An important tradition at the Fair was the ox roasting which was first mentioned in recorded history in 1799 when Robert Hobbes took his fiancée Betsy Ashford to see the Bull Roast. The ox roasting has always proved to be a popular feature of the event and no less than eight oxen and twelve pigs were roasted in 1909.

The open roast in Rother Street, and integral part of the opening ceremony for Stratford-upon-Avon Mop Fair. Although beef is traditional, pigs have also been roasted at the Mop throughout its history.

A group of well-groomed young men enjoy a spin on Deakin's Dodgems during the 1965 Mop Fair at Stratford-upon-Avon. This alloy machine travelled as Deakin's number 2 Dodgem set.

A Swedish import makes a strange sight at Stratford-upon-Avon's 1979 Mop Fair. The Cinema 180 featured motion themed films projected onto a hemispherical screen, giving the paying public the impression that they were part of the action.

A view down Rother Street for Stratford-upon-Avon's 1959 Mop Fair. In view are: Bob Wilson's Autodrome, J. Ayers' Slip (Helter Skelter), F. and T. Wilson's Waltzer and Bagnall's (ex Pat Collins') Caterpillar.

Riders holding tight on William Barker's Ark, captured at Rugby's 1956 Summer Fair. The Ark is a mixture of animals, bikes and chariots, and was purchased that year by W. Barker. As the evening closed in machines such as these would provide focal points for locals to congregate and experience the latest sounds amplified under the canopy roofs. Leeson often listed the Rock 'n' Roll classics that were enjoying regular play on these machines.

Stevens' visit to Pingle Fields, Nuneaton, photographed 2 May 1964 from the elevation of the railway bank.

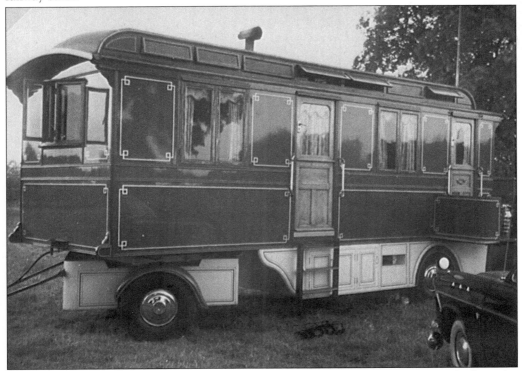

Arthur Armstrong's Living Wagon at Hillmorton Wakes. The wagons were parked on the Watts Lane site and visited by Leeson on 26 June 1959.

Joe Gandey of Gandey's Circus photographed 1 September 1965 on Rugby Cattle Market. Leeson records a conversation with Mr Gandey in which he was shown an autographed brochure presented by the Duke of Bedford to Mr Gandey during an earlier stay at Woburn.

Two
Northamptonshire

Jack Leeson was a native of the Northamptonshire village of Long Buckby, and it was the three annual fairs there that kindled what was to become his lifelong interest. Then, as now, the fairs were held in the streets of the village, a setting that undoubtedly made such periodic incursions seem more dramatic in a young boy's eyes. Visits to the nearby county town would have provided similar excitement, with annual fairs held on open spaces such as Midsummer Meadow and the Old Racecourse. Kettering Feast at the start of July still occupies an important place in the county's calendar of fairs, and has been run by the Thurston family for over a century now. Daventry was once notable for having three Mop Fairs in successive weeks during October; now, not one remains. Interestingly, Daventry represents the eastern limit of the use of the name Mop, the nickname for a hiring fair that is peculiar to a certain part of the English Midlands. At Rothwell the tradition of its Trinity Monday Fair (known locally as 'Rowell Fair') is still jealously guarded, with the ceremony of the reading of the fair's charter attracting a huge crowd of onlookers at six o'clock in the morning.

The 'back' of Kettering Feast Fair where all the Living vans were parked, taken by Leeson as he passed by on the train, 30 June 1962.

Two little boys looking at the camera, perhaps wondering when they will be able to ride the Dodgems behind them. This photograph was taken in August 1950 at Long Buckby Feast, Northamptonshire.

Here we are again at Long Buckby, twenty-four years later, at the October Fair in 1974. Both photographs show how close the Fairs were to buildings, reflecting the close relationship between the Fairground and local communities.

Ten years separate this photograph from the one below it, both taken at Long Buckby. This one was the May Fair in 1951, showing Juvenile Swing Boats...

...while this one is taken at Long Buckby Feast, August 1961, and shows a close-up of Gordon Abbott in his Roll Ups Stall, where many a fairgoer tried his or her luck trying to get the balls in the holes to win a prize.

S. Thurston's huge Mack tractor – registration JMJ660 – pulling into town with its Swirl loads on its way to Northampton Midsummer Meadow, 7 May 1961. Thurston's were famous for their Mack tractors and Diamond T tractors.

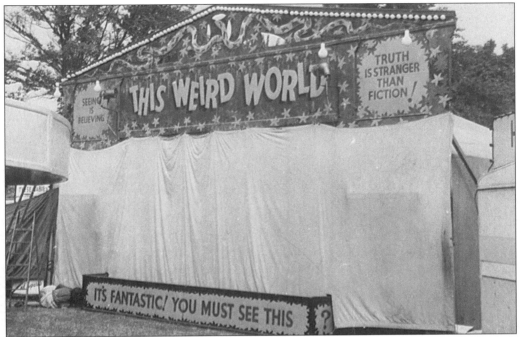

No fair is complete without its selection of sideshows, much more prevalent in past years than today. This Weird World show is owned by J. Appleton, seen at Northampton Whit Fair, 5 June 1965; the show is still sheeted, adding to the mystery and excitement of what might be inside.

Henry Thurston's Rockets, taken 15 July 1961 at Northampton Victoria Park. A lever inside each Rocket enabled the rider to go higher: many an unwitting novice rider was left stranded going around the bottom whilst the others were zooming round high above.

Billy Smart's Southern and Co. Ltd made Living Trailer – registration LYL783 – at Northampton Race Course, 11 June 1961.

Northampton Easter Fair, 15 April 1960. The Fair was based on the Midsummer Meadow site and the photograph illustrates the impressive and imposing presence of the factory chimneys behind.

Boxing was very popular on the Fairground, having its origins back in the prizefighting era in the 1700s. This is a photograph of the famous Pat McKeowen Boxing show, taken at Northampton Easter Fair on the Midsummer Meadow site, 31 March 1961 (which was Good Friday). Pat's parents, Sam and Esther McKeowen also travelled boxing shows and the great Freddie Mills Light, Heavyweight Champion of the World in 1948, started on their show.

W. Thwaite's Juvenile wheel has been built up next to the Big Wheel on the Midsummer Meadow site at Northampton Easter Fair, seen on 27 March 1964, ensuring that the children don't miss out on the fun.

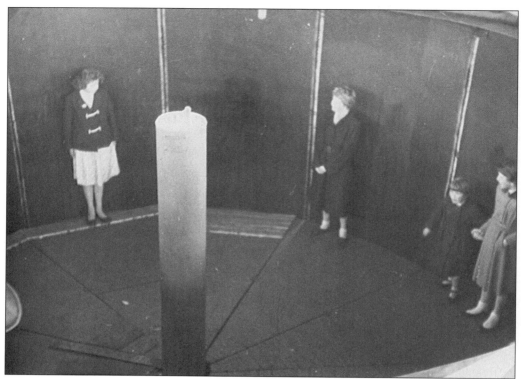

A rare interior photograph showing fairgoers on the drum of C. Thurston's Rotor, waiting for it to begin at Northampton May Fair, Midsummer Meadow site, 2 May 1959.

A long shot of Kings Heath Recreation Ground which was hosting Northampton May Fair, 8 May 1971.

We can just see the head of Mrs Josie Whyatt in the paybox of Stanley Thurston's Ben Hur Ark here, so called after the MGM film, which illustrates not only how much Ben Hur caught the popular imagination but also how the fairground reflects the likes of the public.

The Northampton May Fair, Midsummer Meadow site, taken from across the River Nene, 2 May 1959. We can just see S. Thurston's FWD lorry on the left.

Allan Downs' juvenile Peter Pan Railway,
22 October 1955, taken Daventry Mop
Fair. The Railway, an oval track
measuring about 24ft by 15ft, had been
made by Allan Downs and his sons.

The posters advertising the coming of the
Fair are always eye-catching and bold.
This one, advertising the Daventry Mops
and bearing the legend '1,000 Smiles An
Hour', was photographed on 16 October
1962.

A close-up of a carved peacock on Allan Downs' Gallopers, which you can just see behind his Peter Pan Railway opposite. As is evident from this picture, it wasn't only horses that were found on these roundabouts.

Landmarks of Northamptonshire tower above J. Whyatt's Octopus at Daventry Mop Fair on the High Street, on 16 October 1962.

The line of shows at the Fair was often the busiest place as people crowded to see what new wonders there were to be seen. Kettering Feast Fair exhibited Mrs T. Allen's Crocodile Girl and Chimpanzee Family shows, photographed 30 June 1962.

Nipper Appleton's Ghost Train is seen here at Kettering Feast Fair, 1 July 1978. Ghost shows were one of the earliest forms of entertainment and always proved popular, as does the Ghost Train ride of today.

Another of Leeson's great shots taken from a moving train! This photograph shows Kettering Feast Fair, 30 June 1962. It takes in almost all of the fair and the houses behind while capturing the comings and goings of visitors who, as we see at the bottom left of the photograph, are either reluctantly leaving or rushing towards the excitement.

E. Holland's ornate Cake Walk was one of many that delighted fairgoers for years as they negotiated its quirky moving gangways. Such sections can be found in modern day funhouses. This is at Rothwell, 7 June 1952. Kettering Feast is always held on the first Saturday after 29 June and is synonymous with the Thurston family who have been attending the event for over a hundred years.

This is also Rothwell, this time on 23 May 1970.

The church has long been associated with the fair with many of the original events celebrated on feast days. Rothwell Charter Fair is a moveable feast associated with the Feast of the Holy Trinity. Owen's New Book of Fairs for 1783 informs us that horses and horned cattle were sold on Trinity Monday, with pedlary all week and leather sold on the last day only. This photograph was taken in 1962.

J. Whiting's Ark, The Chaser, at Rothwell, 20 May 1978.

A view of a beautifully painted living wagon, formerly S. Thurston Senior's and, when the photograph was taken on 8 August 1967, belonging to Henry J. Thurston. It is seen at Bassetts Close, Wellingborough.

Thurston's living wagon (above) was part of the Wellingborough Fair – this photograph shows Harry Parrish's Swirl being built up at the same fair.

Three
Oxfordshire

Oxfordshire occupies a special place in the fairground calendar. At the city of Oxford, on 'the first Monday after the first Sunday after the 1st of the month', the St Giles' Wake Fair signals the start of the travelling showmen's busy autumn season. Held along the broad thoroughfare of St Giles, the fair owes something to both Town and Gown. The tolls on the west side of the fair are collected by the Corporation: those on the opposite side go to St John's College, owners of the Manor of Walton, the original holder of the rights of the fair. A week later the showmen converge on the blanket-making town of Witney for the two days of the annual Feast Fair, exchanging the streets of the county town for the Leys, a pleasant tree-lined open space alongside the parish church. Many of the same showmen will be reunited just over a month later for the Michaelmas Fair at Banbury, held in the town centre on the Thursday after 12 October. In the weeks between, Oxfordshire is a hive of activity with fairs taking place in the streets of Chipping Norton, Woodstock (the first Tuesday in October) and Thame, which has two fairs in quick succession.

P. Cole's Gondolas seen at Oxford St Giles Fair on 4 September 1960. Oxford St Giles Fair is held on the first Monday following the first Sunday after the feast of St Giles (September 1) and lasts for two days. Owen's New Book of Fairs of 1783 lists three fairs for Oxford including one which falls on the Monday after St Giles, September 1. The fair itself is historically divided between the 'college' and the 'city' side, with the college side tracing its rights to the fair from the Manor of Walton. The west side of the fair falls beyond these boundaries and as the fair expanded in the Victorian period, the Markets and Fairs Committee took the initiative of collecting the tolls for this area. This practise is still maintained today under the co-ordination and management of the Property and Leisure Department.

Thame Street Fair, on High Street, showing a variety of machines (Jets and Twist) and a rather mischievous looking boy grinning at the camera, 18 September 1965.

With the look of a local market, this is also Thame Fair on 18 September 1965.

The Galloping Horses have been a firm favourite with fairgoers throughout the years. This ride, seen on 18 September 1965 at Thame, is surrounded by parents waiting for their children to come off. The Pettigrove family had this ride built by Norwich engineer Robert Tidman at the turn of the century.

W. Nichols' Jets ride at Thame with the Town Hall clock tower looming over it, 18 September 1965.

The 'test your strength' Strikers were a common feature of many fairs, as young men lined up to impress their friends in a friendly competition, and indeed they can still be seen on modern fairs. The hammer is almost as big as the lady holding it in this picture, taken at Bloxham Steam Fair and Rally, 27 June 1970.

The people surrounding this set of Gallopers is again testimony to the popularity of this ride which seems to evoke nostalgia in all of us. The beautifully carved and painted effects are clearly visible on Jimmy Williams' ride when it appeared at Bloxham Steam Fair and Rally, which took place on Bloxham fields, 27 June 1971.

Before the fair can be built up, terms have to be legally agreed – these are the Corporation's Regulations for Banbury Michaelmas Fair, posted in Bridge Street, October 1961.

Jones Brothers' Cyclone Twist being built up for Banbury Michaelmas Fair in front of the Crown Hotel.

A photograph showing the sheer size of the Big Wheel on Banbury High Street at the Michaelmas Fair, October 1967. If you ran out of money for the rides, the bank was only a stone's throw away, as long as your money was in Barclays.

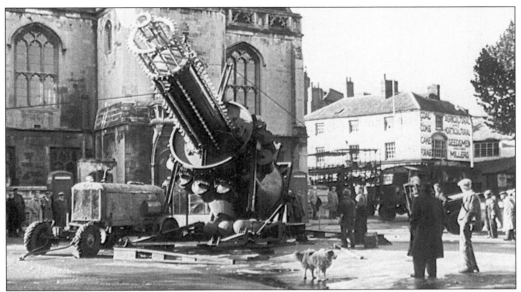

Raising the centre of the Vampire Jets ride was not an easy task – it was a delicate operation involving winch cables from two Matador trucks attached to the Jets' centre and stakes driven into the ground to prevent the centre from moving towards one of the trucks. Once in position, one truck pulls in while the opposite truck lets the winch out. After about half an hour, the centre has moved from its tilted position to an upright position. This photograph was taken the day before Banbury Michaelmas Fair, 17 October 1961. Leeson hadn't visited Banbury since 1957 and he notes that this was his first sight of the new railway station which was being worked on during his last visit.

Not many people know, or even think about, how a ride is built – this photograph shows merely the pole truck of A. Price's Paratrooper with not an umbrella in sight! It was taken in Banbury before the Michaelmas Fair, October 1964.

The ornately carved centre of Bob Wilson's Gallopers with its centre pole matching the symmetry of the clock tower behind, being prepared for Banbury Mop Fair.

Decorative art is a major part of the fairground. The painting on the front boards of R. Wilson's Autodrome, built up on the street as part of Banbury Mop Fair, gives a real feeling of speed and movement.

J. Ayers' Helter Skelter is being built up here as part of Banbury Mop Fair. In a little while the bottom ring, which you can see being laid here, will be transformed into a towering construction offering wonderful views of the town to the fairgoer before he or she goes spiralling back down to earth.

The Traylen Brothers' Helter Skelter at Banbury Mop Fair in October 1954. Notice how much taller it appears to be than the buildings behind.

John Thurston's Waltzer at Oxford St Giles Fair on a very busy day for the Fair in September 1955.

A general view of Oxford St Giles Fair, 4 September 1960, showing Traylen Brothers' Helter Skelter (pictured on p. 57) on the right and their Big Wheel on the left.

What goes up must come down!
G. Webb's Dive Bomber at Oxford
St Giles Fair, 4 September 1960.
The building behind has an 'Army
Information Service' sign on it.

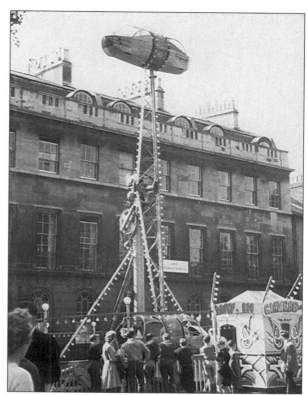

Taken on the same day as the
photograph opposite, this is the
other side of the main street at
Oxford St Giles Fair.

W. Nichols' Speedway Ark at Oxford St Giles Fair showing off the new decor by Hall and Fowle, 4 September 1960. The Ark was built by Lakin's in 1934.

Another very popular ride, W. Nichols' Dodgem at Oxford St Giles Fair, 4 September 1960.

A fantastically painted Boxing Stadium owned by Jack Gage, appearing at Oxford St Giles Fair, 4 September 1960. Boxing shows have long been associated with travelling fairs. Jimmy Wilde, the World Flyweight Champion in 1916, Joe Beckett, the British Heavyweight Champion in 1919, Tommy Farr who narrowly lost to Joe Louis in 1937 and Randolph Turpin are just a few of the famous names who started their careers on the boxing booths. The boxers would line up on the front of the show to take on the challengers from the crowd who could win a purse of £10 if they succeeded in knocking out the professional fighters. However, by the 1960s the British Boxing Board of Control had limited the appearance of professional boxers appearing on fairground shows to three three-minute exhibition bouts and no longer could a would be champion 'catch the gloves' from the crowd and say that they had fought a former Champion of the World.

Charles Thurston's Diamond T tractor – registration CCL205 – waiting to pull into St Giles for the 1965 fair.

Traylen Brothers' six wheel ex-WD Scammell tractor – registration THX764F – with the Helter Skelter load, pulling on at Oxford St Giles Fair, 7 September 1969.

The centre of Pettigrove Brothers'
Gallopers, standing behind the steeted
organ track, is dwarfed by the tower of the
church of St Mary Magdalene at
Woodstock on 3 October 1965.

Harvey's children's roundabout building up
at Woodstock with the Baptist Chapel in
the background, 3 October 1965.

Witney Feast Fair with the church spire in the background, 12 September 1965.

In modern culture the name Frankenstein has become synonymous with Frankenstein's monster rather than with Dr Frankenstein himself, and the Fairground is no exception, as seen by G. Chadwick's Frankenstein's Castle Funhouse at Witney Feast, 11 September 1967.

Four
Gloucestershire

East of the Severn, Gloucestershire is dominated by the Cotswold Hills. Situated on the highest point of the Cotswolds, Stow-on-the-Wold is noted for its two annual horse fairs in May and October. Although fairground amusements are no longer present at these events, trading in horses continues unabated on the appointed days. Further north along the ancient Fosse Way, Moreton-in-Marsh has two fairs, in April and September, that stand perilously close to this busy highway. In the south of the county, the town of Chipping Sodbury celebrates the vernal and autumnal equinoxes with fairs that close the main street. At Chipping Campden, that gem of a market town made rich by the medieval trade in wool, the one-day Scuttlebrook Wake takes place on the Saturday after the Spring Bank Holiday. The biggest of the county's fairs, Tewkesbury Mop, takes over the street of the town centre on 9 and 10 October. During the same month, depending on the vagaries of the calendar, as many as three Mops in succession can be held at Winchcombe. July is festival time in the county, with funfairs adorning Cheltenham's Montpellier Gardens and Gloucester's city centre park.

Tommy Gardner's Juvenile Horses tucked into The Oldbury at Tewkesbury Mop Fair, October 1965.

All stops to Sandford Meadows, Cheltenham. Youngsters ride the engine on J. Coneley's Juvenile Train during the 1964 Summer Fair.

Percy Cole's Gondolas are a fine example of the rewards of preservation – this machine was made in 1888 by Frederick Savage of King's Lynn and remains open to the public to this day. Seen here in 1964 at Cheltenham's Montpellier Gardens.

The Heal Brothers were busy showmen in the Gloucestershire area. This interior view shows Charles Heal's modern alloy Dodgem at Sandford Meadows for the May Fair, 1964.

CHARLES HEAL & SONS

CARNIVAL AND FUN FAIR

Super DODGEMS

SANDFORD MEADOWS, OLD BATH ROAD., CHELTENHAM
WED. MAY 13th to SATURDAY 23rd.
Open Nightly at 6p.m. and Saturday, & Holidays at 2p.m.

A cavalcade of thrills can be glimpsed in Heal's eye-catching poster for the 1964 Fair. Machines present included Heal's Twist, Big Wheel, Ark, Dodgem and Swirl, with Sanders' Octopus in support.

Bobby Edwards Jnr's MG sports car with his sisters, left to right: Edie, Lily, Queenie and Dolly. They are seen here at Stow-on-the-Wold Fair on 11 May 1936.

Stow-on-the-Wold Market Place gives way to R. Edwards & Sons' Amusements for the October Fair, 1964.

Winchcombe Mop Fair, 9 October 1965.

Chris Morris' Ark draws a crowd at Winchcombe Mop. This Jackson Ark travelled throughout the Midlands during its twenty-two year ownership with the Morris family. After spending a couple of years in Ireland it now travels Scotland with Benny Codona.

A favourite landmark at any fair: Howard's Lighthouse Slip seen at Tewkesbury Mop, 1965.

Stalls line Barton Street for Tewkesbury Mop, 1965.

At the far end of Barton Street access to the town is barred by W. Harris' Twist.

Danter's Jackson Waltzer positioned in Spring Gardens for Tewkesbury Mop, 1965. This machine was later sold to Maurice Rowland who has always travelled in the West Country.

Mothers and babies browse Appleton's Spotted Lady and Mexican Twist Shows at Cirencester Carnival, July 1964.

Held in a field off Gloucester Road, Cirencester Carnival proves a popular event. For 1964 R. Edwards provided his first class amusements with the Swirl, Monte Carlo Rally, Ark and Dodgem in attendance. Children were catered for with Edwards' fine Austin Car Track.

Gloucester Park Fair normally enjoys the best of the British summer. Percy Cole's Gondolas provide a trip back in time for visitors in 1964.

Modern thrill rides in the form of Henry Rogers' Waltzer, Sid Stocks' Calypso, R. Henderson's Dive Bomber, C. Wynn's Rotor and Sheppard's Big Wheel fill out the ground for the 1964 Gloucester Park Fair.

Chipping Sodbury Mop Fair, 1965. George Rogers' Ark and Dodgem and Percy Rogers' Big Wheel provide the amusements.

Getting ready for the Scuttlebrook Wake Fair at Chipping Campden, June 1969. W. Kimberley's Dodgem track is being unloaded.

Hatwell Brothers' AEC Matador – registration DBW231 – drawing into Chipping Camden for the 1969 Wake Fair.

Following closely behind Hatwell Brothers' AEC Matador (seen on the previous page) is their Foden tractor – registration JXA667.

A fleet of transport second to none – R. Edwards & Sons' ERF tractor and box truck brings the Ark loads into Chipping Camden for the 1969 Wake Fair.

Hatwells' Gallopers at Moreton-in-Marsh Spring Fair, 1965. A Walker machine, built in 1911, it was acquired by the Hartwell Brothers in 1941, who used it at the Oxfordshire 'Holiday at Home' Fairs during the Second World War.

Alongside Hatwells' Gallopers stands another venerable attraction, the Royal African Jungle shooting gallery.

A general view of Moreton-in-Marsh's Spring Fair, April 1965. This photograph shows the amusements stretched out alongside the Fosse Way, looking south.

Building up for the 1964 Autumn Fair in Moreton-in-Marsh. W. Kimberley's Albion flat lorry – registration HDU147 – carries the plates and sleepers for his Dodgem track.

Five
Herefordshire and Worcestershire

The neighbouring counties of Herefordshire and Worcestershire, separated by those most ancient of hills, the Malverns, entertain a variety of fairs each year. At the foot of the hills, on the eastern side, Malvern Link Common has been the scene of fairs since the introduction of bank holidays in the late nineteenth century. The railway station on the edge of the common provided day-trippers from Birmingham and the Black Country with the opportunity of a breath of fresh air and all the fun of the fair. On the opposite side of Worcestershire, the village green at Broadway is the scene of the annual Wake Fair in the week of the Spring Bank Holiday. Pitchcroft, Worcester's riverside racecourse, has been the site of many fairs over the years. Evesham still has its Mop Fair in the town centre on the Friday following Michaelmas Day. Apart from Ledbury Mop, Herefordshire has no autumn fairs. In this county the hiring fairs took place during the month of May, when a lull in the farming year was the chance for a day of recreation. Of many such fairs along the Marches St Ethelbert's Fair at Hereford was, and still is, the most important. The city also enjoyed an Easter Bank Holiday Fair for much of the twentieth century.

Bertie Ayers' Lighthouse Slip sends a clear message to pedestrians and motorists alike – the fair is in town! Evesham Mop is seen here on 9 October 1965.

Billy Watkins' Waltzer caters for the small crowds at his fair on the local sports field at Pershore in April 1964. This Waltzer, a conversion from an Ark, was a popular machine in this region, and survives into the present even though it is now based in Ireland.

Ted Ormond, who travelled often with the late Billy Watkins, leaning on the mudguard of Billy's Foden tractor at Pershore in April 1964.

Billy Watkins' square-ended Dodgem track patronized by a more orderly customer than those at Stratford-Upon-Avon Mop Fair in 1965 (see p. 21). It is seen here at Pershore fair, April 1964.

Getting ready for the next ride – customers wait on the steps of Billy Watkins' Dodgem track at Pershore, 1964.

An overview of the fair at Pershore on 25 April 1964. Billy Watkins' Waltzer is seen flanked by various juvenile rides and round stalls.

A smart juvenile Austin Car Track and set of Swing Boats photographed at Pershore Fair, April 1964.

Broadway Wake Fair as seen from the main road through the village, May 1964 ...

... and the village green seen from the other end. Behind John Hartwells' children's ride on the left of the picture, stands W. Kimberley's Dodgem track.

Worcester Easter Fair with J. Sheppard's Chairoplanes visible in the centre of the picture, 1965.

Billy Watkins' makes an adjustment to his Scammell tractor – registration HDW460 – on Pitchcroft at Worcester Easter Fair, 1965.

Brett's new Maxwell Waltzer (without front boards) provides the thrills at Hill's Easter Fair at Hereford. Leeson records the venue as St George's Playing Field in April 1965.

Equally popular at the same venue is G. Rogers' Lakin Speedway Ark, boasting a full set of new motorcycles.

Malvern Link Fair dwarfed by the Worcestershire Beacon.

Travelling away from home but advertising a full complement of amusements: Arthur Armstrong's eight-wheel Foden flat lorry at Malvern Link, August 1964.

Sid Squires' Lakin Ark: a busy Midlands traveller seen here at Malvern Link, August 1964.

Arthur Armstrong's Bennett type Twist seen here at Malvern Link. The Twist ride was initially named after the popular dance routine, with later models such as this being called 'The Cyclone' in an attempt to appeal to those seeking a faster thrill ride.

J. Sutton's compact alloy Dodgem track photographed at Malvern Link Fair, August 1965.

Alf Peters' Dodgem track and Gallopers at the 1933 Malvern Link Fair.

H. Harvey's square-ended Dodgem track at the August 1964 Malvern Link Fair. Leeson notes that the track was an early Orton model previously belonging to R. Gale.

Six

Leicestershire

The honour of holding the last major fair of the year falls to the Leicestershire town of Loughborough. It is here, starting on the second Thursday in November, that the showmen open their amusements for what is, for most of them, their last engagement of the season. The November Pleasure Fair was granted by Henry III in 1228, and in the more than seven centuries since then it has always occupied the Market Place and surrounding streets. Leicester's May Fair, granted in 1473, has not proved so enduring. Since Jack Leeson recorded it, the fair has fallen into disuse. A similar fate has befallen the Christmas Fair (albeit a relatively modern event), held within the confines of the city's Granby Halls. The Statute fair (or 'Stattis' as it is locally known) at Ashby-de-la-Zouch however still maintains its yearly presence in Market Street each September. The market town of Hinckley, famous for knitted goods, once had two important fairs, in May and August. The former is still kept, but the Statute fair on 26 August has now disappeared. It had the unique distinction of being mentioned in Shakespeare's Henry IV Part II.

Loughborough Street Fair, 1960, a classic back-end fair coming in November that used to signal the end of the travelling season. This view, taken from the top of Billy Williams' Skyscraper Slip, looks towards the Market Place and shows John Farrar's Lakin Waltzer. Loughborough Fair utilizes every available space by providing a maze of stalls, shows, juvenile rides and large rides throughout the town's streets and open spaces. Like any Charter Fair, Loughborough has a rich and varied history and in the words of Henry Morley, a nineteenth century historian, reveals 'the unwritten story of the history of the people'. The original Charter was granted in 1221 and pertained to an annual event on the 31 of July. This was reaffirmed seven years later and extended to cover three days around the Feast of St Peter. A third Charter was further granted a year later in 1228 by Henry III to Hugh Le Despenser Lord of the Manor of Loughborough and related to the Feast of All Souls. The changes to the Calendar introduced in 1752 resulted in the loss of eleven days and the date of the fair became 13 November. However, in 1881 local officials obtained an order to stipulate that the opening day of the Fair would always fall on the second Thursday in November and the date has since remained constant.

Albert Holland, Frances Holland and young Albert Holland seen in their Living Wagon at Lutterworth Feast, August 1958.

Albert Holland's living wagon, seen from the outside at Lutterworth Feast, 1959.

A typical Leicestershire village fair – Lutterworth Feast on Clarke's Meadow, 5 August 1967.

Albert Holland and Henessey, his St Bernard dog, photographed on 16 August 1958 at Lutterworth Feast.

Real rifles for pretend cowboys: John Bibb's Winchester Saloon Shooter are seen at Leicester May Fair which was held on the Saffron Lane ground and is seen here on 29 April 1961.

Local interest in the bizarre and grotesque – crowds gather around Billy Kayes' Largest Rat Show and Temple of Death at Leicester May Fair, 1961. Showmen regularly re-themed their shows to sustain the novelty factor, and Leeson notes that the Temple of Death had recently travelled as the Shemara Jungle Girl Show.

Bert Holland's Maxwell Waltzer lights up Leicester Granby Halls for the Christmas Fair, 1959.

Mrs A. Holland's 20th Century Dodgem provides entertainment at Leicester Granby Halls, Christmas 1959.

George Godden poses with Mrs Norman and Jim Norman in their hoopla stall at Leicester Stadium car park, August 1958.

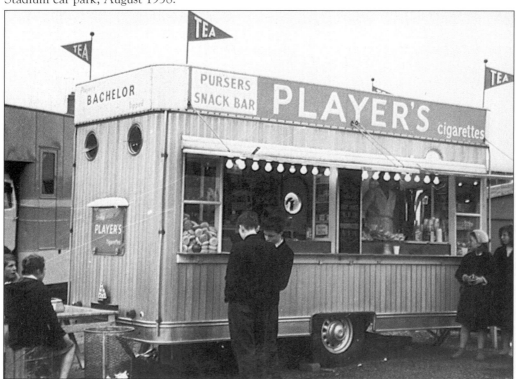

George Purser's mobile refreshment trailer provides tea and cigarettes at Leicester May Fair, Saffron Lane, 1961.

A rare appearance of 'The Air Aces' at Leicester May Fair, 1958. The Air Aces were a motor cycle trick act known as the Australian Flying Aces. The wording on their publicity leaflet held in the National Fairground Archive states 'The most thrilling, sensational and spectacular display of high powered aerobatics ever performed in a British arena. Hurling through space at terrific speeds the "Aces" introduce an entirely new conception of machine and man artistry. The "Air Aces" present the world's only somersaulting motor cycle act and rider at 35 feet above ground level. A life time of thrills in every performance'. The show toured all over the world during the 1950s including South Africa in 1952/3, Germany in 1954 and the United Kingdom in 1955 and 1958.

Ashby-de-la-Zouch Statutes is another famous back-end street fair. This picture of Elias Harris' Lang Wheels Jets was taken 25 September 1965.

At the other end of Market Street at Ashby-de-la-Zouch Statutes is Richards' Cake Walk complete with fairground organ.

Turville's Dalek Juvenile at the May 1966 Melton Mowbray Steam Fair and Traction Engine Rally.

Vintage machinery, in the shape of Ashley Brothers' Gallopers and Harry Lee's Steam Yachts, adds an authentic old time feel to the 1965 Melton Mowbray Steam Fair and Traction Engine Rally.

Hinckley Statutes Fair, August 1964. Bagnall's Waltzer is visible in the centre of the picture.

W. Bagnall's Lang Wheels Dodgem attracts good crowds at Hinckley May Fair, 1964.

Sheppard's Big Wheel provides the aerial thrills at Hinckley May Fair, 1964.

Known as the original Waltzer, J. P. Collins' Lakin machine pulls in the crowds at Hinckley May Fair, 1964.

A landmark of Loughborough Fair – Henry Warwick's Shooter tucked into the 'Golden Fleece' yard on Granby Street. Photographed by Leeson in November 1960, he notes that the stall has stood here for fifty-three years. Loughborough Fair features groups of rides on the Market Place, the Cattle Market, Devonshire Square, Bedford Square and Ward End. The connecting streets in between are lined with round stalls, sideshows and juvenile rides.

November drizzle deters the punters at the 1959 Loughborough Fair. This photograph shows the selection of machines on the Market Place, including Farrar's Waltzer, Thurston's Swirl, Butlin's Helter Skelter and Wynn's Rotor.

The scene above shows better weather a year later in November 1960 in Devonshire Square. Bagnall's Caterpillar, a popular ride of the time, is on the left.

Dense fog gave way to winter sunshine in November 1963, as Leeson stands on the steps of Arthur Holland's Ark to capture the view away from Bedford Square.

Good weather again in November 1965 as J. Noyce's Gallopers and W. Williams' Big Wheel pack into Devonshire Square.

Armstrong's machines dominate Ward End in November 1958. Amidst the drizzle can be seen Arthur Armstrong's Dodgem, Henry Armstrong's Caterpillar and Raymond Armstrong's Waltzer.

A night shot of the Market Place in November 1959 with Charles Thurston's Jets, Wynn's Rotor and Butlin's Helter Skelter lighting up the winter sky.

Immaculate as ever: Noyce's Gallopers on the Market Place in November 1962.

Ready to rotate: these riders look unsure of what to expect on J. Williams' Looper. This novelty ride appeared on the Market Place in November 1963.

Seven

Coventry

There was a time when many households in Coventry waited for the arrival of the Great Fair each Whitsun to buy their crockery, linen goods and linoleum. All could be found at bargain prices among the stalls of the 'Pot Fair', the large market that stood alongside the amusements. The fair dates from the days when Coventry was one of the four most important cities in England. Granted by charter in 1218 as an eight-day Trinity Fair, it became known as the Great or Corpus Christi Fair. Although trade was its original purpose it was always an important festival in the city. In the late fourteenth century the nationally-famous Coventry plays were performed during the week of the fair. Three centuries later the legendary figure of local heroine Lady Godiva was incorporated into the proceedings of the fair when the Godiva Procession was instituted. Such was the fame of the Great Fair then that it became the magnet for the London theatrical companies, who abandoned their stages in the capital to mount performances in Coventry during Trinity Week. Once held in the streets of the city, the Great Fair now takes place on Hearsall Common over the week of the Spring Bank Holiday. Although the market has diminished in its appeal, the display of amusements has lost none of its vigour.

Showmen's ties with local councils go far back, as is shown in this photograph of the Civic Opening of Coventry Whit Fair by Councillor Winslow Lord Mayor of Coventry cutting the tape on Hearsall Common, 24 May 1958.

A view of Allan Downs' Chairoplanes in motion, taken on Hearsall Common at Coventry August Fair, 2 August 1960. Notice the child sat on the grass on the left of the picture gazing on and the operator sat in the middle of the machine.

B. Parkin's unusual Juvenile space ships taken at Hearsall Common, 6 August 1959. B. Parkin and R. Armstrong are in the paybox in the centre of the photograph.

A front view of N. Roberts' Ghost Train, which he has also intriguingly called Tunneux D'Amour, taken at Coventry Easter Fair, Hearsall Common site, 18 April 1960. This formerly belonged to J. W. Harris but now his name has been painted out and replaced with 'GHOST TRAIN'.

This is also taken at Hearsall Common, but it is Coventry Pot Fair on 16 May 1959. Jack Leeson took this photograph from the top of the Rotor, looking north.

Fairground lad leaning nonchalantly against the post waiting for the punters to come and ride E. Pratley's Monte Carlo Speedway, appearing at Coventry Hearsall Common, 6 August 1959.

An old fashioned looking Living Wagon belonging to C. Houltby, taken Hearsall Common at the Coventry Pot Fair, 16 May 1959.

On the same day as the previous two photographs (16 May 1959) also at Coventry Pot Fair, this general view shows living wagons of all shapes and sizes, again taken by Leeson from the top of the Rotor, but this time looking south west.

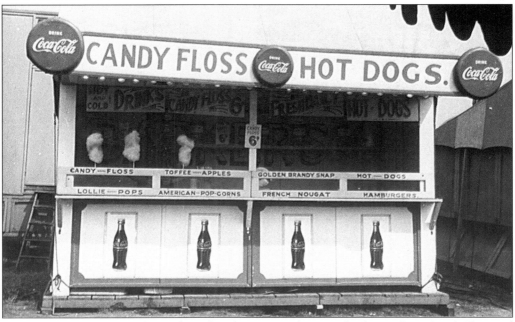

The popularity of Coca Cola is reflected in this strange photograph of T. Barker's Candy Floss and Hot Dogs stall, taken at Coventry August Fair, Hearsall Common site, on 2 August 1960.

A wonderful view of Coventry August Fair as it builds up on Hearsall Common looking far off into the distance and the city beyond, 2 August 1961.

One of the most exciting things about the Fair and Circus is their actual arrival in town. This is the arrival of Billy Smart's Circus in Coventry, parading through the streets with performers on a tractor, 2 October 1959.

Not much of a freak, this tame sheep from Chadwick's Animal Freak Show appeared at Coventry Carnival Fair on the Memorial Park site, 18 June 1960.

E. Monte's Hell's Drivers Wall of Death, with spieling in progress, at Coventry Carnival Fair, Memorial Park site, 13 June 1959.

Mrs H. Bishton and her son at their Cake Walk paybox at Hearsall Common, Coventry August Fair, 10 August 1962.

A close-up of Jones Brothers and friends in a Waltzer Car, taken at the Memorial Park site at Coventry Carnival Fair, 14 June 1958.

Ted Pratley and his son standing proudly in front of Pratley's 6-wheel Foden lorry – registration ENV465 – and trailer at Hearsall Common, 25 July 1960. Also in the photograph are Allan Downs and his two daughters. The fairground vehicles were often painted as brightly as the rides themselves and, if you can imagine, this lorry was painted red (wings, radiator and chassis) with a maroon cab.

A Scammell Showtrac lorry – registration KDH141 – belonging to the famous Pat Collins standing next to his Waltzer at Coventry Carnival Fair on the Memorial Park, 13 June 1959. This view is looking south.

The front boards of Billy Shufflebottom's Wild West Show advertising the various and often dangerous acts inside, seen here on Hearsall Common at Coventry Whit Fair, 24 May 1958.

Eight
Birmingham

Until 1875 Birmingham's two great fairs, the Whitsuntide Fair and the Michaelmas Onion Fair, were held in the Bull Ring and the surrounding labyrinth of streets. In that year the town council (Birmingham had yet to become a city) banned the fairs because of 'rowdiness'. Undaunted by this ban, the showmen migrated to the neighbouring, and then separate, village of Aston. Here the tradition of the fairs was continued on a piece of ground known as the Old Pleck. In later years the fairs moved to the Serpentine, land lying between the parish church and Aston Villa Football Club's ground. The fairs were held under the banner of the great Walsall-based showman Pat Collins, and under his direction they more than maintained their old popularity. The fairs ceased in 1968 when the Serpentine was sold for development. Pat Collins also had an interest in Sutton Park, a popular weekend resort for Birmingham folk. From the early years of the twentieth century he had a lease of the Crystal Palace part of the park and ran a permanent fair there until 1962. In Birmingham itself, the use of the city's parks for fairs was encouraged during the war years. From the late 1950s Cannon Hill Park was the site of the Tulip Festival, an event supported by a large funfair run by local showman Bob Wilson.

An evocative view of the entrance to Birmingham Onion Fair at Aston Serpentine which frames a Big Wheel on the left and is dominated by W. Williams' Skyline Slip (Helter Skelter) on the right, 1 October 1960.

A general view of Birmingham Onion Fair which Leeson took from the top of a Helter Skelter, capturing the dominance of the Big Wheel as it towers over the Aston Serpentine site, 29 September 1962. Behind the left of the Wheel you can see a hazy factory and tall industrial chimneys to the right.

A close up of E. Harris' Octopus car in full flight, at Birmingham Onion Fair, 2 October 1954.

A unusual show, L. T. Howard's 'Satan's Queen of Sex', taken at Birmingham Carnival Fair being held on the Aston Serpentine site, 28 October 1961.

Night-time is when the fair really came alive, but night shots are not that easy to get. This is Birmingham Carnival Fair at dusk, where the lights are just starting to come on, showing Butlin's Helter Skelter, Williams' Dive Bomber in the foreground and Jones Brothers' Big Wheel with its star shaped bulbs. This picture was taken on the Aston Serpentine site, 31 October 1959.

A head-on view of one of the horses of J. J. Collins' Gallopers taken at Birmingham Onion Fair, 28 September 1957. Leeson notes that this three-abreast Gallopers had no organ and also that it was a glorious day!

F.C.S.F. members Messrs F. Richardson, R. Newbold and G. Cornfield posing in front of J. P. Collins' FWD tractor – registration MRE997 – at the Aston Serpentine site for Birmingham Whit Fair, 23 May 1959.

Pat Collins' engines surrounded by a group of fairground enthusiasts from the British Fairground Society and the Friendship Circle of Showland Fans, taken at Birmingham Onion Fair, 1 October 1955. Such societies meet regularly and play a large part in documenting ride and transport details, helping to build up a written history of the fairground. The Friendship Circle of Showland Fans was founded in 1941 by Father Greville and continued until 1967. Its quarterly journal *The Merry-go-Round* contained articles and photographs pertaining to the history of fairs with the enthusiasts building up large photographic collections. The late Jack Leeson was a member of this society.

Slips, or Helter Skelters, can make impressive photographs. This is Pat Collins' taken on the Aston Serpentine site at Birmingham Onion Fair in September 1953.

Often full of weird and wonderful shows, the Birmingham Onion Fair at Aston Serpentine site on 23 May 1959 was showing Billy Kayes' 'Largest Rat in the World' show, which Kayes repeatedly allowed to 'escape' causing panic and invariably grabbing the headlines in the local papers.

A group photograph taken outside the Bates' living wagon at Lightwoods Park in Birmingham. This picture includes: Mrs T. Bates, Mr and Mrs Morgan and daughter, John and Jean Bates and Jacqueline Wilson.

Williams Brothers' Dive Bomber, a thriller of a ride, in action with the boom horizontal at the Aston Serpentine site, Birmingham Carnival Fair, 3 October 1959.

Holding a fair is not just a case of turning up on a ground; it is all co-ordinated with local councils down to the last detail by the lessee or showman who is organizing the event. Once agreed, the fair can be advertised, like this publicity poster for Pat Collins' Birmingham Onion Fair, September 1963.

Pat Collins' Jack and Jill slide on Sutton Park, Sutton Coldfield, 16 July 1955. Imagine the competitions as you raced against your opponent on the opposite slide!

The fountain in Sutton Park at Sutton Coldfield with Pat Collins' Chairoplanes in action over the other side, taken July 1957.

C. Morris' Cyclodrome Thriller Ark Speedway, populated by motor bikes and loud music, taken at Radley's Recreation Ground in Sheldon, 26 September 1964. The ride is surrounded by fairgoers leaning on the barriers waiting for the moment when the platform slows, signalling the beginning of the great rush to secure the 'fastest' bikes, usually on the outside.

The inside of a Monte Carlo, or Speedway, also belonging to C. Morris and taken at Radley's Recreation Ground in Sheldon, 28 September 1963. The Monte Carlo Speedway and Ark Speedway (above) are similar in name only, the one above having evolved out of the old fashioned platform rides whereas this one is a modern ride on a flat track where fairgoers can 'race' each other. Leeson stopped at this fair after visiting the Birmingham Onion Fair.

Bingo is still an old favourite on the fairground. This one, belonging to Chipperfield, was taken at Cannon Hill Park Tulip Festival and Fair on 28 April 1962.

The quaintly named Tulip Express Tram touring the Cannon Hill Park, calling at what Leeson calls 'tastefully made *stations* in various parts of the park', at the Tulip Festival and Fair in April 1961.

Yet another of those side shows that dotted older fairs, here is Sleeping Beauty Alive! at Cannon Hill Park Tulip Festival and Fair, 18 April 1962.

Jack Leeson himself with fellow enthusiast Rowland Scott, who specialized in photographing Lancashire and the North West: Birmingham Carnival Fair, Aston Serpentine site, 29 October 1960.